ois Au

Poetry for Young People

Carl Sandburg

Edited by Frances Schoonmaker Bolin
Illustrated by Steven Arcella

Sterling Publishing Company, Inc.
New York

Dedication

To Andrew, Kara, and Martin Schoonmaker,
"Eager as the great morning."

Acknowledgments

Thanks to Kirsten Wuest and Heidi Grant for their assistance.

A MAGNOLIA EDITIONS BOOK

Editors: Karla Olson, Loretta Mowat
Art Director: Jeff Batzli
Designer: Jennifer Markson
Production Manager: Jeanne E. Kaufman

Library of Congress Cataloging-in-Publication Data

Sandburg, Carl, 1878-1967.
Poetry for young people / Carl Sandburg ; edited by Frances
Schoonmaker Bolin : illustrated by Steven Arcella.
   p. cm.
"A Magnolia Editions book" —T.p. verso.
Includes index.
Summary: Presents a collection of poems by the beloved American
author who, as a young man, travelled across the Midwest as a hobo.
ISBN 0-8069-0818-1
  1. Children's poetry, American [1. American poetry.]
I. Bolin, Frances S. II. Arcella, Steven, ill. III. Title.
IV. Title: Carl Sandburg, poetry for young people.
PS3537.A618A6   1995
811'.52—dc20
                      94-30777
                      CIP
                         AC

"Phizzog," "Rat Riddles," "Landscape," "Summer Grass," and "October Paint" from GOOD MORNING, AMERICA, copyright
1928 and renewed 1956 by Carl Sandburg, reprinted by permission of Harcourt Brace & Company.

"Arithmetic," "Boxes and Bags," "Doors," "Little Girl, Be Careful What You Say," "Sky Talk," and "We Must Be Polite" from THE COMPLETE
POEMS OF CARL SANDBURG, copyright 1950 by Carl Sandburg and renewed 1978 by Margaret Sandburg, Helga Sandburg Crile, and Janet
Sandburg, reprinted by permission of Harcourt Brace & Company.

"Buffalo Dusk," "Jazz Fantasia," and "Summer Stars" from SMOKE AND STEEL by Carl Sandburg, copyright 1920 by Harcourt
Brace & Company and renewed 1948 by Carl Sandburg, reprinted by permission of the publisher.

Photograph p. 3 Courtesy of the Carl Sandburg Collection, Clifton Waller Barrett Library, Special Collections Department, University of Virginia Library

2 4 6 8 10 9 7 5 3 1

Published by Sterling Publishing Company, Inc.
387 Park Avenue South, New York, N.Y. 10016
© 1995 by Magnolia Editions Limited
Introduction © 1995 Frances Schoonmaker Bolin
Illustrations © 1995 Steven Arcella

Distributed in Canada by Sterling Publishing, c/o Canadian Manda Group, One Atlantic Avenue, Suite 105 Toronto, Ontario, Canada M6K 3E7
Distributed in Great Britain and Europe by Cassell PLC, Villiers House, 41/47 Strand, London WC2N 5JE, England
Distributed in Australia by Capricorn Link (Australia) Pty Ltd., P.O. Box 6651, Baulkham Hills, Business Centre, NSW 2153, Australia

Printed in China
All rights reserved
Sterling ISBN 0-8069-0818-1

Contents

Introduction 4

Fog 8

From the Shore 9

Young Sea 10

Last Answers 12

A Sphinx 13

Little Girl, Be Careful What You Say 14

Margaret 14

Arithmetic 17

Plowboy 18

Monotone 19

Phizzog 20

Mask 20

Summer Grass 22

Summer Stars 22

Sky Talk 23

October Paint 25

Theme in Yellow 26

We Must Be Polite 27

Rat Riddles 28

A Homely Winter Idyl 29

Landscape 30

Boxes and Bags 31

Skyscraper 33

Under a Telephone Pole 36

Old Woman 38

Doors 38

A Coin 39

Buffalo Dusk 39

I Sang 40

Jazz Fantasia 43

Window 44

Sheep 44

Between Two Hills 46

Index 48

Restless as a Young Heart, Hunting

CARL SANDBURG WATCHED A THICK FOG MOVE FROM THE NEARBY Chicago harbor to settle over the park where he was walking. The year was 1913 and Sandburg, then a journalist for the *Chicago Daily News*, was on his way to interview a judge. Later, as he sat waiting in the judge's office, he pulled a piece of newspaper from his pocket. On it he wrote: "The fog comes on little cat feet, It sits looking over city and harbor on silent haunches and then moves on." (Look closely at page 8 to see how he revised it before it was published.) These few lines became one of his most famous poems.

When thirty-five-year-old Sandburg wrote "Fog," he had already published a small collection of poetry, but was not yet considered a great poet. Even though he had a steady job with the newspaper, he was restless, still trying to decide what to do with his life. Choosing a profession was no easy matter for him because he had so many interests and talents.

Born January 6, 1878, in Galesburg, Illinois, Sandburg was a wanderer who always wanted to try new things and go to new places. By age eighteen, he had held several jobs, including one delivering milk and another delivering blocks of ice to homes and stores. (This was before people had electric refrigerators.) He worked long, hard hours before and after school, and once nearly froze his feet walking four miles to and from the dairy without overshoes. There was no money for them; the twelve dollars a month Sandburg earned went to help his family.

The young Sandburg was not afraid of hard work, but he did not want to settle for work that was not interesting to him. His nose was always in a book, for his sixth grade teacher had told him, "You don't know what good friends books can be till you try them, till you try many of them." He liked to write, too, and his pockets were always full of odd scraps of paper on which he wrote his many ideas. He loved music and experimented with homemade musical instruments such as a willow whistle and a cigar-box banjo. (He once bought a banjo from a pawn shop for two dollars, and paid a quarter for three banjo lessons.) Most of all, Sandburg loved to travel.

For thirty-five years, Sandburg's father, August, worked as a blacksmith's helper for the Chicago, Burlington and Quincy Railroad (C.B. & Q.) ten hours a day, six days a week, with no vacations. His job was to beat hot iron into railroad parts. Sandburg's mother, Clara, worked to keep house for the family. August was serious, stern, and careful with the little money he earned. Clara was cheerful and full of life, and she valued learning. She once spent more than August could earn in a day to buy an encyclopedia for the children.

Both August and Clara came to the United States from Sweden and were proud of their heritage. Sandburg, the second of seven children (two of his younger brothers died when Carl was a teenager), spoke Swedish before he spoke English; but he wanted to be an American and was afraid that being Swedish meant that he was less American. By the time he reached second grade, he had convinced everyone, including his teachers, to call him Charlie instead of Carl. Not until many years later did he use the name Carl again, finally proud of being both Swedish and American.

Because his father worked for the C.B. & Q., Sandburg could get rail passes. When he was eighteen, his father let him take the train to Chicago alone. He walked all over the city, admiring its busy streets and the beautiful Lake Michigan. Little did he know then that Chicago, the powerful and exciting city he had always wanted to see, would become his home and the subject of many of his poems. However, after he came home, he did know that he would never be content to stay in one place and do monotonous work.

The following year Sandburg set out to see the West, becoming a hobo. For about five months he travelled across the United States—usually by train—and worked at odd jobs to support himself. He sang folk songs around a campfire with other hobos and slept under the stars. He worked in the wheat harvest in Kansas, washed dishes in Colorado, and passed up a chance to join the Gold Rush in Alaska. All the while he wrote in his journal, noting unusual bits of language, interesting faces, and the stories and songs of the people he met. He wrote about the many sights, sounds, and smells of the West, which later found their way into his poems. He read everything he could get his hands on, and he wrote about people, the earth, feelings, wishes, and thoughts. He began to experiment with writing many different forms of poetry. In one of his poems, "A Homely Winter Idyl" (see page 29), he tried writing like Emily Dickinson, using meter (a regular rhythm) and rhyme. But he most often returned to free verse, poetry without a predictable rhythm or rhyme.

"I got education in scraps and pieces of many kinds, not knowing they were part of my education," Sandburg wrote. He never went to high school because the family could only afford to send his older sister, Mary. But Mary shared her books with her brother, and he learned enough to be admitted to college. Though he studied hard and was a good student, Sandburg never graduated: instead of taking all the courses required for graduation, he only took classes in which he had an interest.

Sandburg grew up in the prairie country where Abraham Lincoln had lived. Throughout his life, Sandburg heard stories about Lincoln, many of which had never been written down, and he decided to record them. The book was originally intended for children, but he kept writing until there were four big volumes for adults. The books helped many people understand Lincoln as a real person. Later, Sandburg did write a book for children, *Abe Lincoln Grows Up*. He also wrote a collection of folk songs, *The American Songbag*, including ones he sang as a hobo, such as "I Ride an Old Paint," "The John B. Sails," and "Blow the Man Down." As if this were not enough, Sandburg also reviewed movies for the *Chicago Daily News*, and he even became friends with Charlie Chaplin and other stars.

When Sandburg met the pretty and energetic schoolteacher Lilian Steichen, he knew he had found someone who understood him, believed in his talent, and shared his interests. He was thirty years old when they married. Lilian's parents had been immigrants, too, and she convinced him to return to using the name Carl because it seemed more like him. Lilian's family called her "Paus'l," a word used in Belgium to mean someone dear. But Lilian's sister couldn't say Paus'l and called her Paula instead. Sandburg thought that Paula suited her best.

Carl and Paula Sandburg's lives were never free of struggles. They had very little money. Margaret, their first child, had epilepsy, a condition about which little was known and for which there was no medication. In order to earn extra money for medical bills, Sandburg lectured, read poetry, and sang folk songs all over the United States, in addition to his job as a newspaper journalist. Their second child died at birth. Their two youngest, Janet and Helga, were both physically healthy; however, Janet was slow in school, and was hit by a car when she was sixteen, which made her learning problems worse. Neither Margaret nor Janet ever moved away from home.

Sandburg kept writing poetry despite his many hardships. He worked long into the night while Paula cared for the girls. He wrote about people he met and faces he remembered, like the plowboy with a team of horses who made a picture in his mind (see page 18). He wrote about Margaret's blue eyes and little wild wishes (see page 14), the sea pounding the shore (see page 9), and summer grass (see page 22). Sometimes people criticized Sandburg for using free verse, saying it didn't make sense. But Sandburg's work was carefully written and it appealed to ordinary people.

Sandburg was a wonderful storyteller, often telling tales to his daughters. He thought American children needed their own fairy tales, not ones about knights and princesses locked up in castles. He made up stories about simple things that happened in ordinary places to ordinary people like the White Horse Girl and the Blue Wind Boy. He called his *Rootabaga Stories* "nonsense stories with a lot of American fooling in them." Many of his poems contain lines about "fooling" as well, such as "Arithmetic is where numbers fly like pigeons in and out of your head" (see page 17); in "We Must Be Polite" (see page 27), he offers advice about what to do if you meet a gorilla or if an elephant comes to your door.

When he was in his sixties, Sandburg and his family moved to a new home in the mountains of North Carolina with enough room for his books and papers and for Paula and Helga's herd of dairy goats. Helga, who had recently been divorced, lived with them for several years and helped her father with his writing. Sandburg lived in North Carolina until his death on July 22, 1967.

Sandburg received many awards and prizes for his work as a writer and poet. Once asked whether he wanted to be known as a poet, a biographer, or a historian, Sandburg replied that he didn't think it was important what he was called. When a famous reporter asked him what he thought was the worst word in the English language, Sandburg said it was "exclusive," because when you are exclusive you shut people out of your mind and heart. Maybe that is why Carl Sandburg could never settle on one profession and followed his dream of becoming a poet and a writer. Some like to say that he was the eternal hobo—always exploring and trying new things and places—and was never exclusive.

FOG

The fog comes
on little cat feet.

It sits looking
over harbor and city
on silent haunches
and then moves on.

FROM THE SHORE

A lone gray bird,
Dim-dipping, far-flying,
Alone in the shadows and grandeurs and tumults
Of night and the sea
And the stars and storms.

Out over the darkness it wavers and hovers,
Out into the gloom it swings and batters,
Out into the wind and the rain and the vast,
Out into the pit of a great black world,
Where fogs are at battle, sky-driven, sea-blown,
Love of mist and rapture of flight,
Glories of chance and hazards of death
On its eager and palpitant wings.

Out into the deep of the great dark world,
Beyond the long borders where foam and drift
Of the sundering waves are lost and gone
On the tides that plunger and rear and crumble.

grandeurs—*instances of being magnificent*   palpitant—*throbbing, beating*
tumults—*outbursts, commotions*   sundering—*parting, breaking apart*
rapture—*a feeling of intense emotion*   plunger—*to dive*

YOUNG SEA

The sea is never still.
It pounds on the shore
Restless as a young heart,
Hunting.

The sea speaks
And only the stormy hearts
Know what it says:
It is the face
    of a rough mother speaking.

The sea is young.
One storm cleans all the hoar
And loosens the age of it.
I hear it laughing, reckless.

They love the sea,
Men who ride on it
And know they will die
Under the salt of it.

Let only the young come,
   Says the sea.
Let them kiss my face
   And hear me.
I am the last word
   And I tell
Where storms and stars come from.

hoar—*frost*

LAST ANSWERS

I wrote a poem on the mist
And a woman asked me what I meant by it.
I had thought till then only of the beauty of the mist, how
     pearl and gray of it mix and reel,
And change the drab shanties with lighted lamps at
     evening into points of mystery quivering with color.

  I answered:
The whole world was mist once long ago and some day
     it will all go back to mist,
Our skulls and lungs are more water than bone and tissue
And all poets love dust and mist because all the last
     answers
Go running back to dust and mist.

shanties—*little huts or houses*

A Sphinx

Close-mouthed you sat five thousand years and never let
    out a whisper,
Processions came by, marchers, asking questions you
    answered with gray eyes never blinking, shut lips
    never talking.
Not one croak of anything you know has come from your
    cat crouch of ages.
I am one of those who know all you know and I keep my
    questions: I know the answers you hold.

LITTLE GIRL,
BE CAREFUL WHAT YOU SAY

Little girl, be careful what you say
when you make talk with words, words—
for words are made of syllables
and syllables, child, are made of air—
and air is so thin—air is the breath of God—
air is finer than fire or mist,
finer than water or moonlight,
finer than spider-webs in the moon,
finer than water-flowers in the morning:
     and words are strong, too,
     stronger than rocks or steel
stronger than potatoes, corn, fish, cattle,
and soft, too, soft as little pigeon-eggs,
soft as the music of hummingbird wings.
     So, little girl, when you speak greetings,
when you tell jokes, make wishes or prayers,
     be careful, be careless, be careful,
     be what you wish to be.

MARGARET

Many birds and the beating of wings
Make a flinging reckless hum
In the early morning at the rocks
Above the blue pool
Where the gray shadows swim lazy.

In your blue eyes, O reckless child,
I saw today many little wild wishes,
Eager as the great morning.

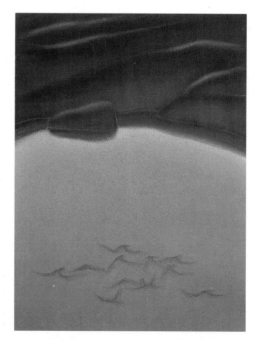

14

ARITHMETIC

Arithmetic is where numbers fly like pigeons in and out of your head.

Arithmetic tells you how many you lose or win if you know how
many you had before you lost or won.

Arithmetic is seven eleven all good children go to heaven—or five six
bundle of sticks.

Arithmetic is numbers you squeeze from your head to your hand to
your pencil to your paper till you get the answer.

Arithmetic is where the answer is right and everything is nice
and you can look out of the window and see the blue sky—or the answer is
wrong and you have to start all over and try again and see how it
comes out this time.

If you take a number and double it and double it again and then
double it a few more times, the number gets bigger and bigger and goes
higher and higher and only arithmetic can tell you what the number is when
you decide to quit doubling.

Arithmetic is where you have to multiply—and you carry the
multiplication table in your head and hope you won't lose it.

If you have two animal crackers, one good and one bad, and you
eat one and a striped zebra with streaks all over him eats the other, how
many animal crackers will you have if somebody offers you
five six seven and you say No no no and you say Nay nay nay and you say
Nix nix nix?

If you ask your mother for one fried egg for breakfast and she
gives you two fried eggs and you eat both of them, who is better in
arithmetic, you or your mother?

PLOWBOY

After the last red sunset glimmer,
Black on the line of a low hill rise,
Formed into moving shadows, I saw
A plowboy and two horses lined against the
    gray,
Plowing in the dusk the last furrow.
The turf had a gleam of brown,
And smell of soil was in the air,
And, cool and moist, a haze of April.

I shall remember you long,
Plowboy and horses against the sky in shadow.
I shall remember you and the picture
You made for me,
Turning the turf in the dusk
And haze of an April gloaming.

gloaming—*twilight*

MONOTONE

The monotone of the rain is beautiful,
And the sudden rise and slow relapse
Of the long multitudinous rain.

The sun on the hills is beautiful,
Or a captured sunset sea-flung,
Bannered with fire and gold.

A face I know is beautiful—
With fire and gold of sky and sea,
And the peace of long warm rain.

monotone—*a single, unchanging sound*
multitudinous—*consisting of a crowd or large*
number of individuals

PHIZZOG

This face you got,
This here phizzog you carry around,
You never picked it out for yourself
        at all, at all—did you?
This here phizzog—somebody handed it
        to you—am I right?
Somebody said, "Here's yours, now go see
        what you can do with it."
Somebody slipped it to you and it was like
        a package marked:
"No goods exchanged after being taken away"—
This face you got.

MASK

Fling your red scarf faster and faster, dancer.
It is summer and the sun loves a million green leaves,
        masses of green.
Your red scarf flashes across them calling and a-calling.
The silk and flare of it is a great soprano leading a chorus
Carried along in a rouse of voices reaching for the heart
        of the world.
Your toes are singing to meet the song of your arms:

Let the red scarf go swifter.
Summer and the sun command you.

rouse—*an excited state of being*

20

SUMMER GRASS

Summer grass aches and whispers.

It wants something; it calls and sings; it pours
  out wishes to the overhead stars.
The rain hears; the rain answers; the rain is slow
  coming; the rain wets the face of the grass.

SUMMER STARS

Bend low again, night of summer stars.
So near you are, sky of summer stars,
So near, a long-arm man can pick off stars,
Pick off what he wants in the sky bowl,
So near you are, summer stars,
So near, strumming, strumming,
  So lazy and hum-strumming.

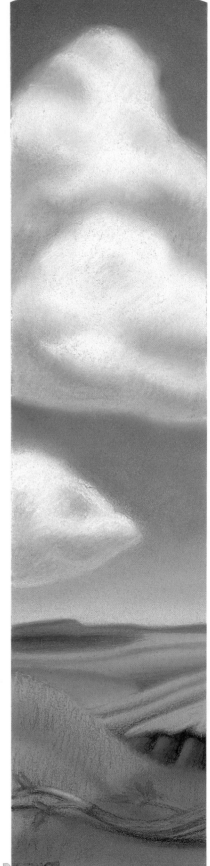

SKY TALK

Wool white horses and their heads sag and roll,
Snow white sheep and their tails drag far,
Impossible animals ever more impossible—
      They walk on the sky to say How do you do?
          Or Good-by or Back-soon-maybe.

Or would you say any white flowers come
          more lovely than certain white clouds?
Or would you say any tall mountains beckon,
rise and beckon beyond certain tall walking clouds?

Is there any roll of white sea-horses equal to
          the sky-horse white of certain clouds rolling?

Now we may summon buyers and sellers
and tell them to go buy certain clouds today,
          go sell other clouds tomorrow,
          and we may hear them report
Ups and downs, brisk buying, brisk selling,
      Market unsteady, never so many fluctuations.

Can there be any veering white fluctuations,
      any moving incalculable fluctuations
      quite so incalculable as certain clouds?

fluctuations—*changes of rising and falling*
incalculable—*not capable of being measured or calculated*

23

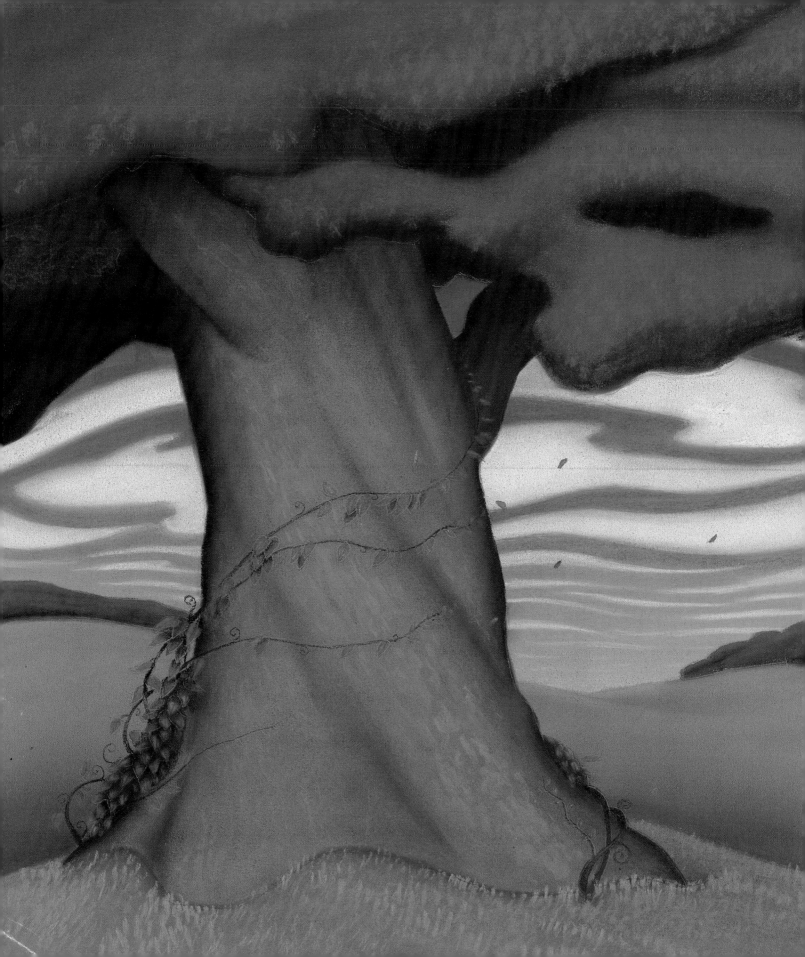

OCTOBER PAINT

Flame blue wisps in the west,
Wrap yourselves in these leaves
And speak to winter about us.
Tell winter the whole story.

Red leaves up the oaken slabs,
You came little and green spats
Four months ago; your climbers
Put scroll after scroll around
The oaken slabs. "Red, come red,"
Some one with an October paint
Pot said. And here you are,
Fifty red arrowheads of leaf paint
Or fifty mystic fox footprints
Or fifty pointed thumbprints.
Hold on, the winds are to come
Blowing, blowing, the gray slabs
Will lose you, the winds will
Flick you away in a whiff
One by one, two by two…Yet
I have heard a rumor whispered;
Tattlers tell it to each other
Like a secret everybody knows…
Next year you will come again.
Up the oaken slabs you will put
Your pointed fox footprints
Green in the early summer
And you will be red arrowheads
In the falltime…Tattlers
Slip this into each other's ears
Like a secret everybody knows.
…If I see some one with an
October paint pot I shall be
Full of respect and say,
"I saw your thumbprints everywhere,
How do you do it?"

THEME IN YELLOW

I spot the hills
With yellow balls in autumn.
I light the prairie cornfields
Orange and tawny gold clusters
And I am called pumpkins.
On the last of October
When dusk is fallen
Children join hands
And circle round me
Singing ghost songs
And love to the harvest moon;
I am a jack-o'-lantern
With terrible teeth
And the children know
I am fooling.

WE MUST BE POLITE
(LESSONS FOR CHILDREN ON HOW TO BEHAVE UNDER PECULIAR CIRCUMSTANCES)

1

If we meet a gorilla
what shall we do?
Two things we may do
if we so wish to do.

Speak to the gorilla
very, very respectfully,
"How do you do, sir?"

Or, speak to him with less
distinction of manner,
"Hey, why don't you go back
where you came from?"

2

If an elephant knocks on your door
and asks for something to eat,
there are two things to say:

Tell him there are nothing but cold
victuals in the house and he will do
better next door.

Or say: We have nothing but six bushels
of potatoes—will that be enough for
your breakfast, sir?

victuals (pronouced VITT-els)—
supplies of food

RAT RIDDLES

There was a gray rat looked at me
with green eyes out of a rathole.

"Hello, rat," I said,
"Is there any chance for me
to get on to the language of the rats?"

And the green eyes blinked at me,
blinked from a gray rat's rathole.

"Come again," I said,
"Slip me a couple of riddles;
there must be riddles among the rats."

And the green eyes blinked at me
and a whisper came from the gray rathole:
"Who do you think you are and why is a rat?
Where did you sleep last night and why do you sneeze
        on Tuesdays? And why is the grave of a rat no
        deeper than the grave of a man?"

And the tail of a green-eyed rat
Whipped and was gone at a gray rathole.

A HOMELY WINTER IDYL

Great, long, lean clouds in sullen host
   Along the skyline passed today;
While overhead I've only seen
   A leaden sky the whole day long.

My heart would gloomily have mused
   Had I not seen those queer, old crows
Stop short in their mad frolicking
   And pose for me in long, black rows.

idyl—*a poem that describes something or tells a story*
mused—*thought about or reflected on something*

LANDSCAPE

See the trees lean to the wind's way of learning.
See the dirt of the hills shape to the water's
    way of learning.
See the lift of it all go the way the biggest
    wind and the strongest water want it.

BOXES AND BAGS

The bigger the box the more it holds.

Empty boxes hold the same as empty heads.

Enough small empty boxes thrown into a big empty box fill it full.

A half-empty box says, "Put more in."

A big enough box could hold the world.

Elephants need big boxes to hold a dozen elephant handkerchiefs.

Fleas fold little handkerchiefs and fix them nice and neat in
      flea handkerchief boxes.

Bags lean against each other and boxes stand independent.

Boxes are square with corners unless round with circles.

Box can be piled on box till the whole works comes tumbling.

Pile box on box and the bottom box says, "If you will kindly take
      notice you will see it all rests on me."

Pile box on box and the top one says, "Who falls farthest if or
      when we fall? I ask you."

Box people go looking for boxes and bag people go looking for bags.

SKYSCRAPER

By day the skyscraper looms in the smoke and sun and
      has a soul.
Prairie and valley, streets of the city, pour people into it
      and they mingle among its twenty floors and are
      poured out again back to the streets, prairies and
      valleys.
It is the men and women, boys and girls so poured in and
      out all day that give the building a soul of dreams
      and thoughts and memories.
(Dumped in the sea or fixed in a desert, who would care
      for the building or speak its name or ask a policeman
      the way to it?)

Elevators slide on their cables and tubes catch letters and
      parcels and iron pipes carry gas and water in and
      sewage out.
Wires climb with secrets, carry light and carry words,
      and tell terrors and profits and loves—curses of men
      grappling plans of business and questions of women
      in plots of love.
Hour by hour the caissons reach down to the rock of the
      earth and hold the building to a turning planet.
Hour by hour the girders play as ribs and reach out and
      hold together the stone walls and floors.
Hour by hour the hand of the mason and the stuff of the
      mortar clinch the pieces and parts to the shape an
      architect voted.
Hour by hour the sun and the rain, the air and the rust,
      and the press of time running into centuries, play on
      the building inside and out and use it.

Men who sunk the pilings and mixed the mortar are laid
      in graves where the wind whistles a wild song without
      words.
And so are men who strung the wires and fixed the pipes
      and tubes and those who saw it rise floor by floor.

Souls of them all are here, even the hod carrier begging
          at back doors hundreds of miles away and the brick-layer
          who went to state prison for shooting another
          man while drunk.
(One man fell from a girder and broke his neck at the end
          of a straight plunge—he is here—his soul has gone
          into the stones of the building.)
On the office doors from tier to tier—hundreds of names
          and each name standing for a face written across with
          a dead child, a passionate lover, a driving ambition
          for a million-dollar business or a lobster's ease of life.

Behind the signs on the doors they work and the walls tell
          nothing from room to room.
Ten-dollar-a-week stenographers take letters from corporation
          officers, lawyers, efficiency engineers, and tons of
          letters go bundled from the building to all
          ends of the earth.
Smiles and tears of each office girl go into the soul of the
          building just the same as the master-men who rule
          the building.

Hands of clocks turn to noon hours and each floor empties
          its men and women who go away and eat and come
          back to work.
Toward the end of the afternoon all work slackens and all
          jobs go slower as the people feel day closing on them.

One by one the floors are emptied.... The uniformed
          elevator men are gone. Pails clang...Scrubbers
          work, talking in foreign tongues. Broom and water
          and mop clean from the floors human dust and spit,
          and machine grime of the day.
Spelled in electric fire on the roof are words telling miles
          of houses and people where to buy a thing for
          money. The sign speaks till midnight.

Darkness on the hallways. Voices echo. Silence holds.
　　　…Watchmen walk slow from floor to floor and try
　　　the doors. Revolvers bulge from their hip pockets.
　　　…Steel safes stand in corners. Money is stacked in them.
A young watchman leans at a window and sees the lights of barges
　　　butting their way across a harbor, nets of red and white
　　　lanterns in a railroad yard, and a span of glooms
　　　splashed with lines of white and blurs of crosses
　　　and clusters over the sleeping city.
By night the skyscraper looms in the smoke and the stars
　　　and has a soul.

grappling—*struggling with*
caissons—*box-like structures used in constructing underwater or in*
　　　　working below the earth near a large body of water
stenographers—*office workers employed to take notes*

35

Under a Telephone Pole

I am a copper wire slung in the air,
Slim against the sun I make not even a clear line of
    shadow.
Night and day I keep singing—humming and thrumming:
It is love and war and money; it is the fighting and the
    tears, the work and the want,
Death and laughter of men and women passing through me,
    carrier of your speech,
In the rain and the wet dripping, in the dawn and the
    shine drying,
              A copper wire.

OLD WOMAN

The owl-car clatters along, dogged by the echo
From building and battered paving-stone;
The headlight scoffs at the mist
And fixes its yellow rays in the cold slow rain;
Against a pane I press my forehead
And drowsily look on the walls and sidewalks.

The headlight finds the way
And life is gone from the wet and the welter—
Only an old woman, bloated, disheveled and bleared.
Far-wandering waif of other days,
Huddles for sleep in a doorway,
Homeless.

welter—*rolling or tossing, turmoil*
disheveled—*having mussed up clothing*
bleared—*dimmed, blurred*
waif—*orphan*

DOORS

An open door says, "Come in."
A shut door says, "Who are you?"
Shadows and ghosts go through shut doors.
If a door is shut and you want it shut,
   why open it?
If a door is open and you want it open,
   why shut it?
Doors forget but only doors know what it is
   doors forget.

A COIN

Your western heads here cast on money,
You are the two that fade away together,
　　Partners in the mist.

　　Lunging buffalo shoulder,
　　Lean Indian face,
We who come after where you are gone
Salute your forms on the new nickel.

　　You are
　　To us:
　　The past.

　　Runners
　　On the prairie:
　　Good-by.

BUFFALO DUSK

The buffaloes are gone.
And those who saw the buffaloes are gone.
Those who saw the buffaloes by thousands and how they
　　　　pawed the prairie sod into dust with their hoofs,
　　　　their great heads down pawing on in a great pageant
　　　　of dusk,
Those who saw the buffaloes are gone.
And the buffaloes are gone.

sod—*earth, dirt*
pageant—*elaborate display*

I Sang

I sang to you and the moon
But only the moon remembers.
  I sang
O reckless free-hearted
                 free-throated rhythms,
Even the moon remembers them
And is kind to me.

JAZZ FANTASIA

Drum on your drums, batter on your banjoes,
sob on the long cool winding saxophones.
Go to it, O jazzmen.

Sling your knuckles on the bottoms of the happy
tin pans, let your trombones ooze, and go husha-
husha-hush with the slippery sand-paper.

Moan like an autumn wind high in the lonesome tree-
tops, moan soft like you wanted somebody terrible,
cry like a racing car slipping away from a motorcycle
cop, bang-bang! you jazzmen, bang altogether drums,
traps, banjoes, horns, tin cans—make two people fight
on the top of a stairway and scratch each other's eyes
in a clinch tumbling down the stairs.

Can the rough stuff…now a Mississippi steamboat
pushes up the night river with a hoo-hoo-hoo-oo…
and the green lanterns calling to the high soft stars
…a red moon rides on the humps of the low river
hills…go to it, O jazzmen.

clinch—*embrace, close hold*

WINDOW

Night from a railroad car window
Is a great, dark, soft thing
Broken across with slashes of light.

SHEEP

    Thousands of sheep, soft-footed, black-nosed sheep—one by one going up the hill and over the fence—one by one four-footed pattering up and over—one by one wiggling their stub tails as they take the short jump and go over—one by one silently unless for the multitudinous drumming of their hoofs as they move on and go over—thousands and thousands of them in the gray haze of evening just after sundown—one by one slanting in a long line to pass over the hill—

    I am the slow, long-legged Sleepyman and I love you sheep in Persia, California, Argentina, Australia, or Spain—you are the thoughts that help me when I, the Sleepyman, lay my hands on the eyelids of the children of the world at eight o'clock every night—you thousands and thousands of sheep in a procession of dusk making an endless multitudinous drumming on the hills with your hoofs.

BETWEEN TWO HILLS

Between two hills
The old town stands.
The houses loom
And the roofs and trees
And the dusk and the dark,
The damp and the dew
   Are there.

The prayers are said
And the people rest
For sleep is there
And the touch of dreams
   Is over all.

Index

A
"Arithmetic," 6, 17

B
"Between Two Hills," 46
"Boxes and Bags," 31
"Buffalo Dusk," 39

C
Chicago Daily News, 4, 6
"A Coin," 39

D
Dickinson, Emily, 5
"Doors," 38

F
"Fog," 4, 8
"From the Shore," 6, 9

H
"A Homely Winter Idyl," 5, 29

I
"I Sang," 40

J
"Jazz Fantasia," 43

L
"Landscape," 30
"Last Answers," 12
"Little Girl, Be Careful What
    You Say," 14

M
"Margaret," 6, 14
"Mask," 20
"Monotone," 19

O
"October Paint," 25
"Old Woman," 38

P
"Phizzog," 20
"Plowboy," 6, 18

R
"Rat Riddles," 28

S
Sandburg, Carl
    books, 6
    childhood, 4
    family, 4–5, 6
    schooling, 5
    travels, 4, 5
    writing, 4, 5, 6
"Sheep," 44
"Skyscraper," 33
"Sky Talk," 23
"A Sphinx," 13
"Summer Grass," 6, 22
"Summer Stars," 22

T
"Theme in Yellow," 26

U
"Under a Telephone Pole," 36

W
"We Must Be Polite," 6, 27
"Window," 44

Y
"Young Sea," 10